Pope Francis

A BOY WHO LISTENED TO GOD

Find our books at Amazon, Barnes & Nobles, Walmart, Books-A-Million, OverDrive, Kobo, Lulu and more!

LIKE, SHARE AND FOLLOW US ON FACEBOOK, INSTAGRAM, PINTEREST, YOUTUBE, LINKEDIN, SPOTIFY, APPLE PODCAST AND MORE!

www.SlothDreamsBooks.com

Text & Illustrations © 2025 by KeriAnne N. Jelinek

All Rights Reserved, including the right of reproduction in whole are in part in any form. Sloth Dreams Books & Publishing and colophon are registered trademarks of Sloth Dreams Books & Publishing Company, LLC.

Published by Sloth Dreams Books & Publishing, LLC.
Sloth Dreams Children's Books
Pennsylvania, USA
www.SlothDreamsBooks.com

All Rights Reserved.
ISBN: 978-4-3644-5083-1

Except in the United States of America, this book is sold subject to the condition that it shall not, by way of trade or otherwise, be lent, re-sold, hired out, or otherwise circulated without the publisher's prior consent in any form of binding or cover other that in which it is published and without a similar condition including this condition being imposed on the subsequent purchaser.

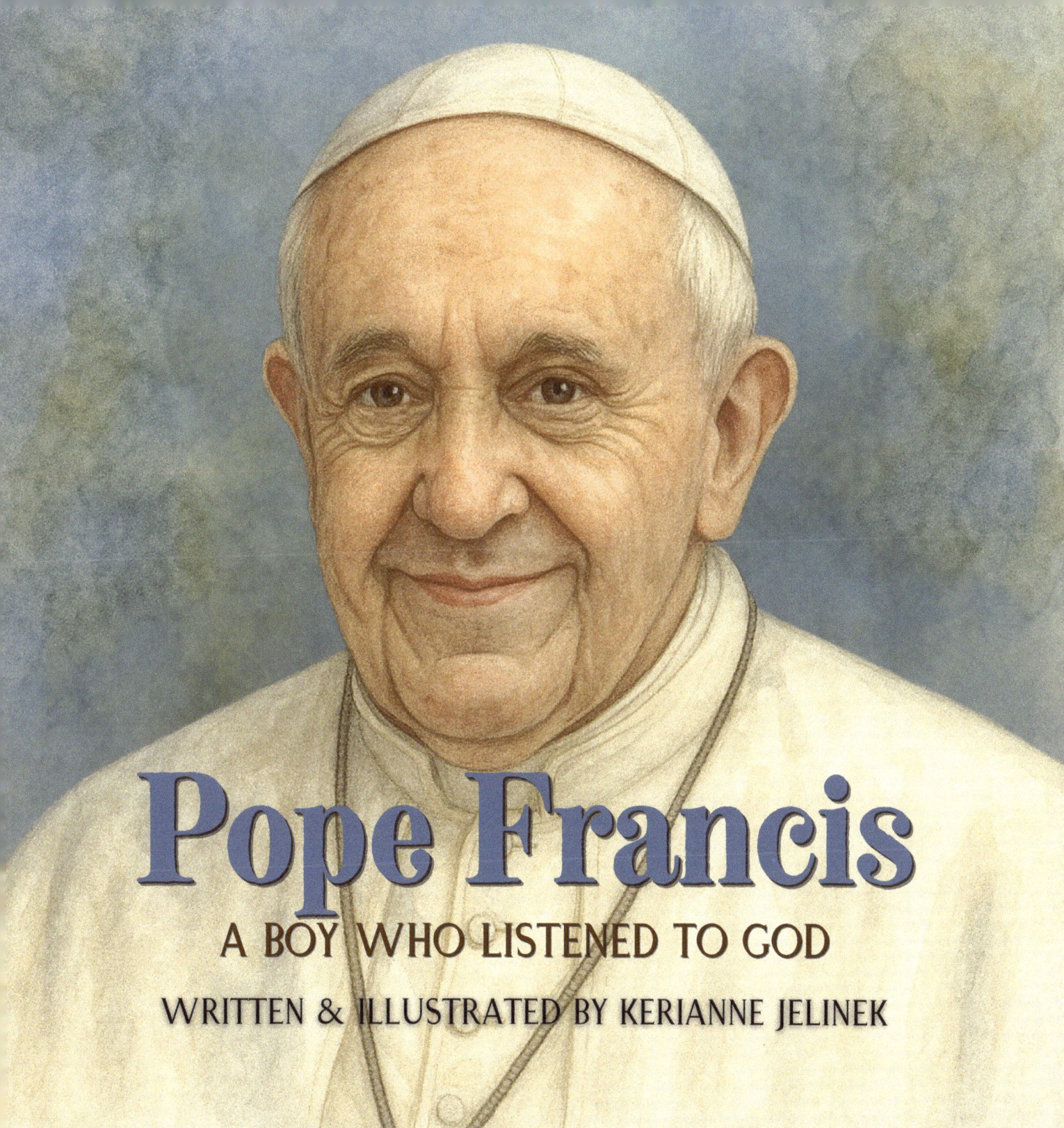

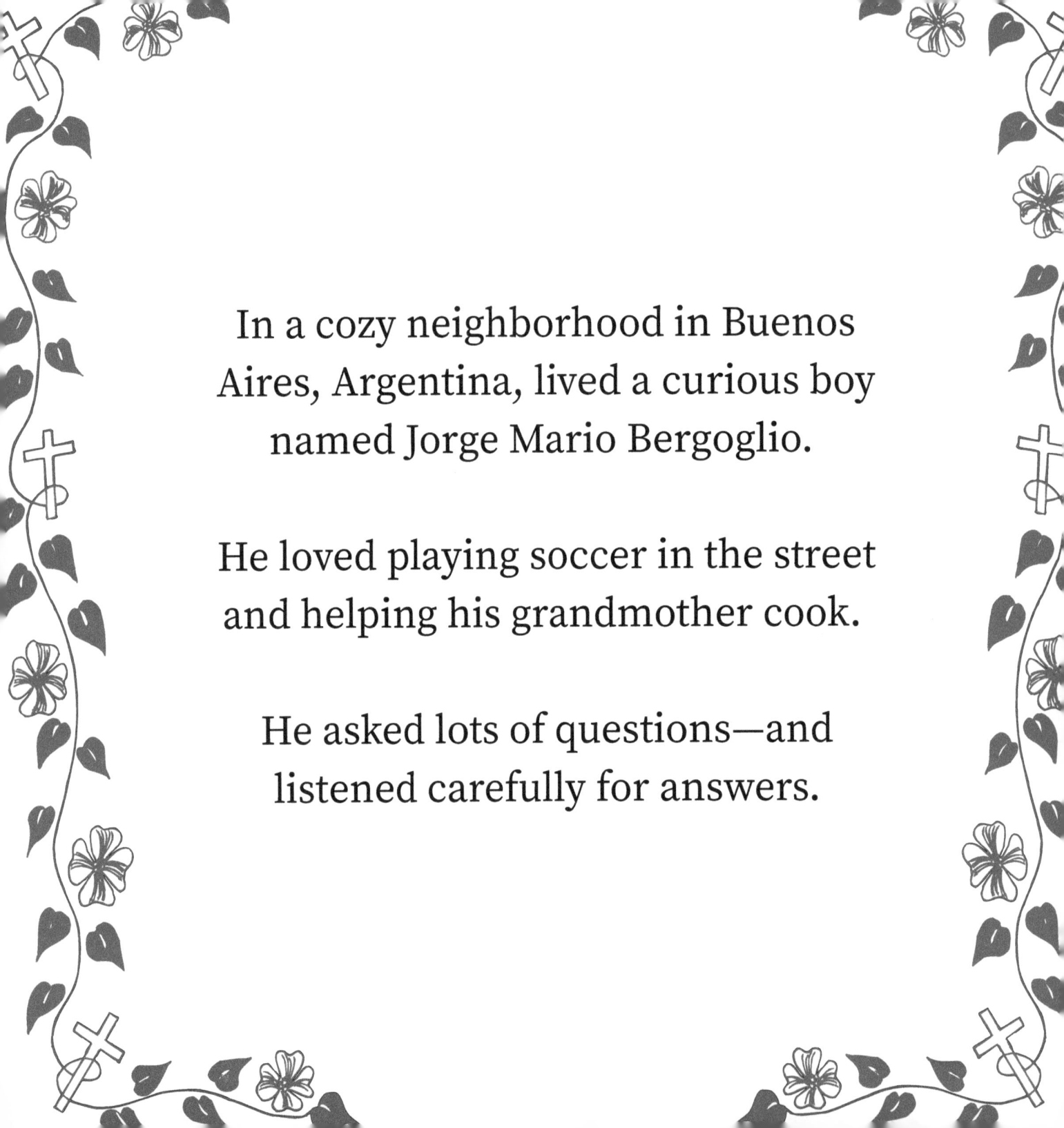

In a cozy neighborhood in Buenos Aires, Argentina, lived a curious boy named Jorge Mario Bergoglio.

He loved playing soccer in the street and helping his grandmother cook.

He asked lots of questions—and listened carefully for answers.

Jorge's family was kind and faithful. Every night, they prayed together.

His father worked on trains, and his mother took care of their five children.

Jorge learned the power of love, family, and helping others.

One day, Jorge gave his sandwich to a hungry boy at school.

"He needs it more than I do," Jorge said.

His teachers smiled. Jorge had a heart full of kindness.

As he grew older, Jorge loved reading books about science, saints, and stories of the world.

At first, he wanted to become a doctor. But soon, he discovered a deeper calling.

When Jorge became very sick as a teenager, he promised God he would live a life of service if he got better.

After he healed, he knew what he had to do—he would become a priest.

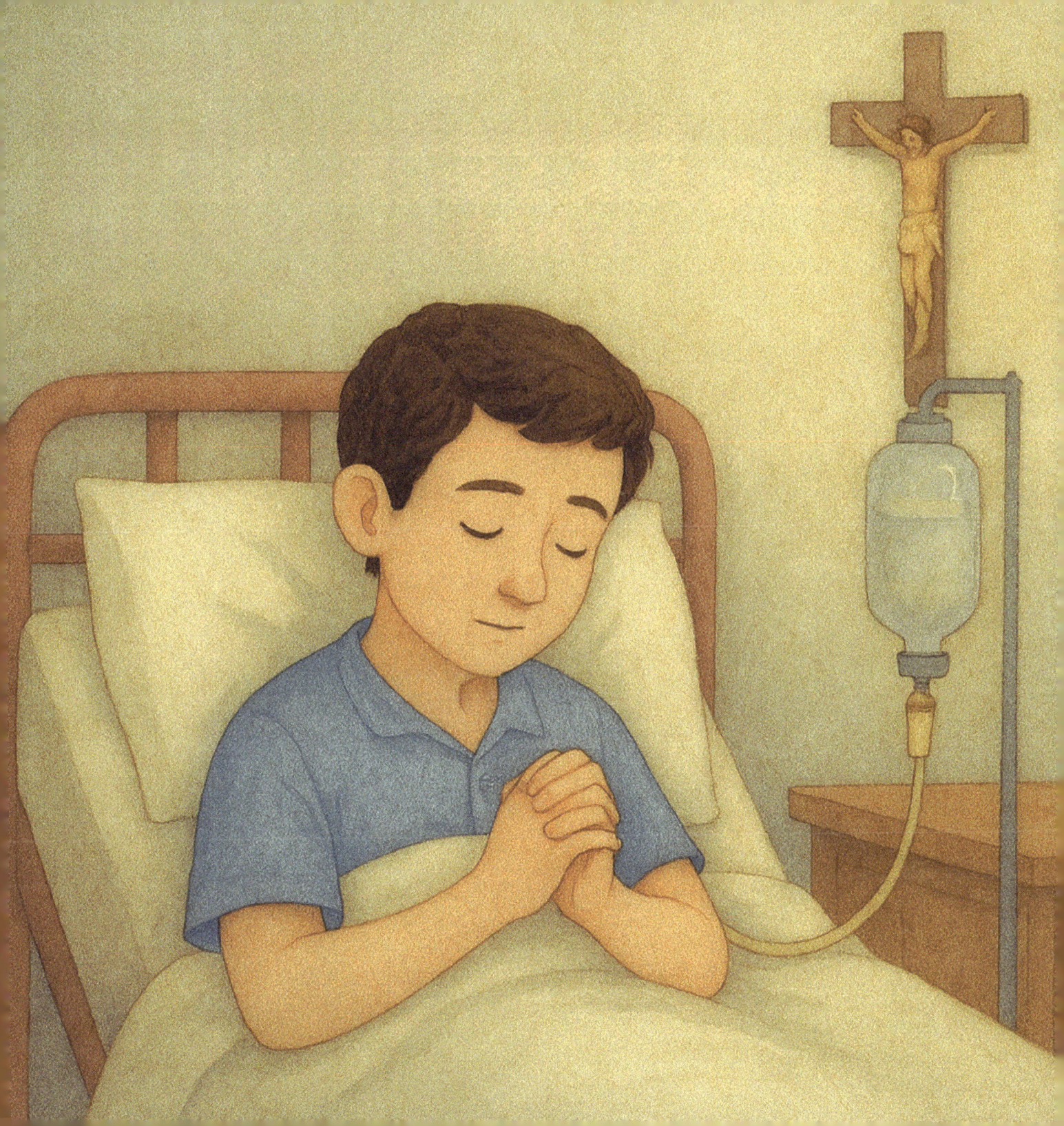

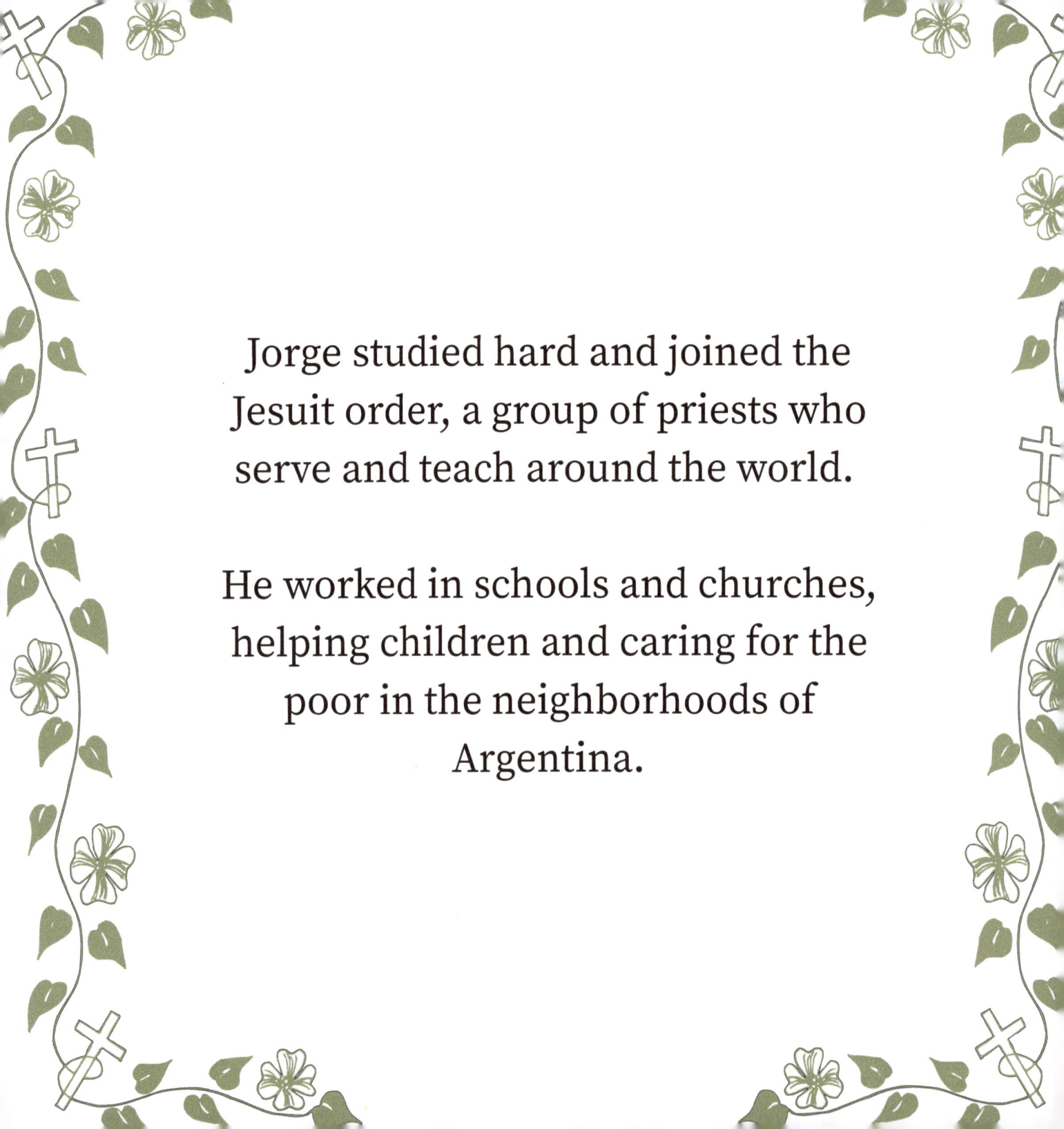

Jorge studied hard and joined the Jesuit order, a group of priests who serve and teach around the world.

He worked in schools and churches, helping children and caring for the poor in the neighborhoods of Argentina.

Even when Jorge became a bishop, he chose to ride the bus and live in a small apartment.

He believed true leaders should be humble, just like Jesus.

In 2013, something incredible happened.

Cardinals from around the world gathered in Rome to choose a new pope.

To everyone's surprise, they chose Jorge—the first pope from South America!

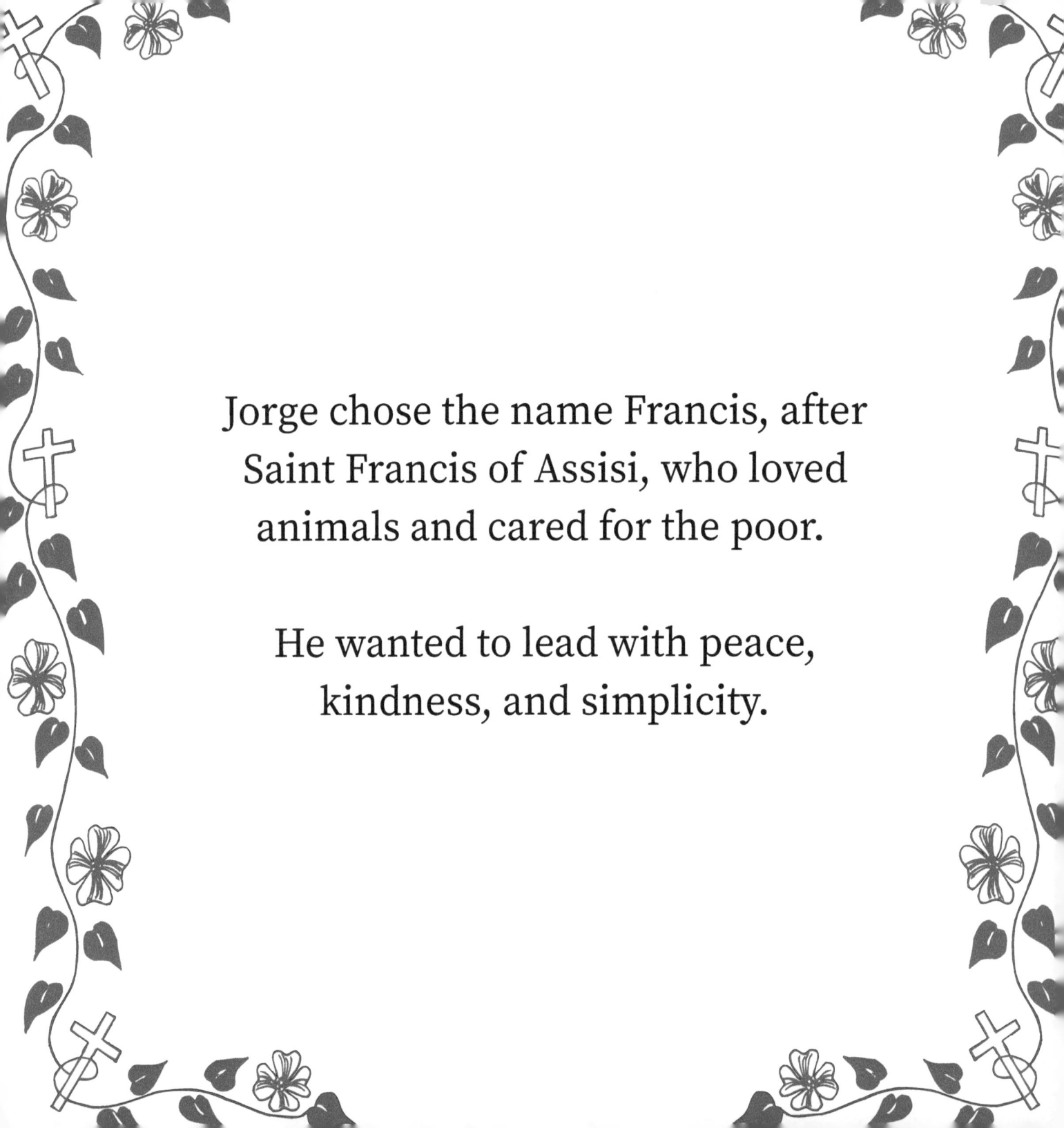

Jorge chose the name Francis, after Saint Francis of Assisi, who loved animals and cared for the poor.

He wanted to lead with peace, kindness, and simplicity.

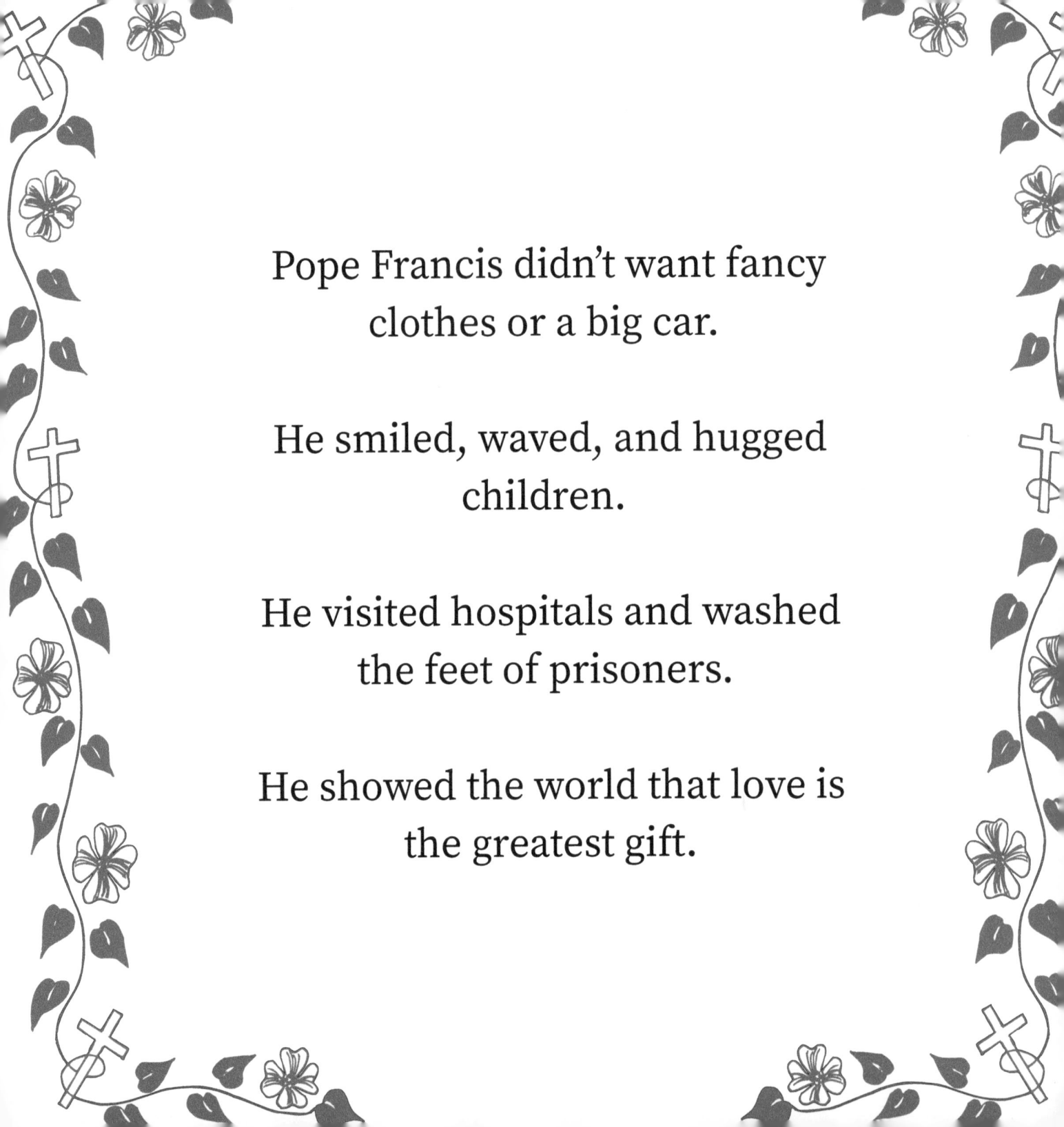

Pope Francis didn't want fancy clothes or a big car.

He smiled, waved, and hugged children.

He visited hospitals and washed the feet of prisoners.

He showed the world that love is the greatest gift.

Pope Francis wrote letters to the world about protecting nature and helping the planet.

"The Earth is our home," he said.

"Let's care for it like a family garden."

He spoke up for people who had no one to speak for them—children, the poor, refugees, and the sick.

"Every person matters," Pope Francis said.

"Everyone is loved by God."

Pope Francis became like a wise grandfather to millions.

He told people to smile, forgive each other, and never stop hoping.

"Joy is a choice," he said.

"Choose it every day."

He taught that we should take care of one another, listen more than we speak, and always walk with kindness.

"God is always near," he reminds us.

"Especially in the quiet and the small."

And so, the story of Pope Francis continues—through every kind word, every gentle act, and every heart that chooses love.

Maybe, just maybe, you'll follow in his footsteps too.

On April 21, 2025, after a long battle with a lung illness, Pope Francis closed his eyes for the last time.

People around the world prayed, mourned his passing, and shared stories of his kindness.

Though he is no longer here, his spirit lives on—in every hug, every smile, and every act of love.

He showed us how to walk in faith, and now, his light shines in our hearts forever.

On April 21, 2025, Pope Francis passed away peacefully at the age of 88. His funeral was held on Saturday, April 26, at 10:00 a.m. in St. Peter's Square, Vatican City, led by Cardinal Giovanni Battista Re. Thousands of people from around the world gathered to honor his life, including leaders and faithful who admired his message of compassion and humility.

In keeping with his wishes, Pope Francis chose a simple funeral. He was laid to rest in a modest wooden coffin, without the traditional triple caskets used for previous popes. Breaking with centuries of tradition, he requested to be buried not beneath St. Peter's Basilica, but in the Basilica of St. Mary Major in Rome. This basilica held special meaning for him; he often visited the icon of the Virgin Mary, known as Salus Populi Romani, seeking comfort and guidance during his papacy. His tomb, marked simply with "Franciscus," reflects his lifelong commitment to humility and service.

As the bells tolled and prayers were whispered, the world said goodbye to a pope who walked with the people, listened with his heart, and taught us all to care for one another.

In Loving Memory of Pope Francis
(Jorge Mario Bergoglio, 1936–2025)

This book is dedicated to the life, love, and legacy of Pope Francis— a shepherd of peace, a friend to the poor, and a grandfather to the world.

May his message of kindness, humility, and hope continue to guide hearts—young and old—
for generations to come.

"Let us protect with love all that God has given us." – Pope Francis

In Loving Memory of Pope Francis
(Jorge Mario Bergoglio, 1936–2025)

This book is dedicated to the life, love, and legacy of Pope Francis—a shepherd of peace, a friend to the poor, and a grandfather to the world.

www.ingramcontent.com/pod-product-compliance
Lightning Source LLC
LaVergne TN
LVHW070218080526
838202LV00067B/6847